This book is dedicated to Rich, Lucas &
Elise,
Thank you for your consistent
encouragement.

I love you.

Printed in the United States of America

ISBN 978-1-7372232-0-7 (Paperback)

ISBN 978-1-7372232-1-4 (Hardcover)

Simon Sheep Faces His Fear

Written by Frances Pinal
Illustrated by Kyle Kaloi

Simon sheep was struck with fear.

He learned of farmer Fred's plan to
have the sheep sheered.

This frightened Simon, he'd never had his wool cut before.

He decided that the only thing to do, was to leave his beloved farm to avoid being sheered.

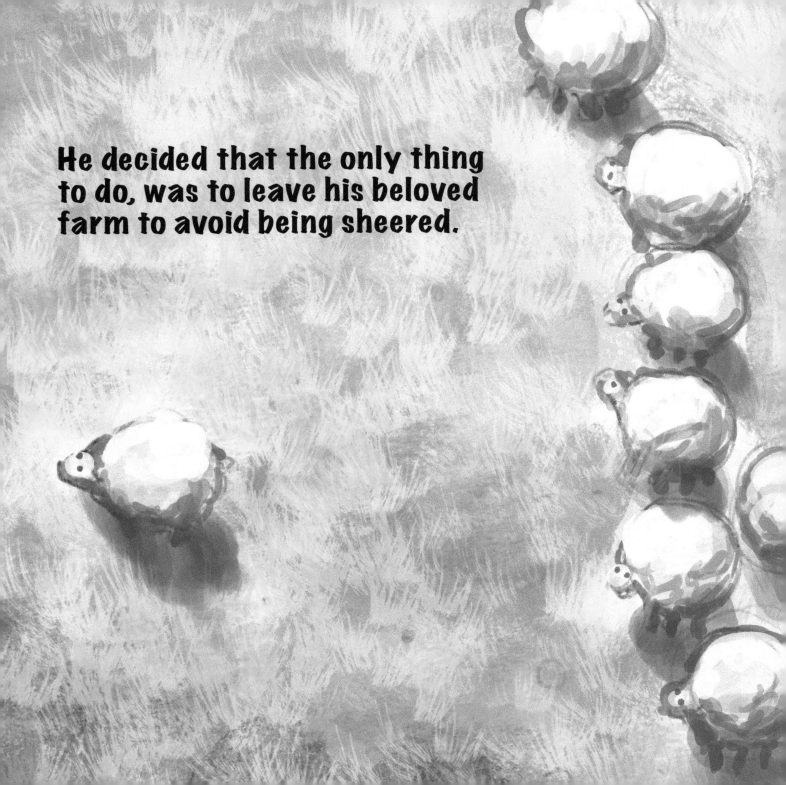

So that same night, while the other animals slept.... he made his escape.

For many days Simon was sad and lonely. He missed all of his friends back at the farm.

Then one day, Davie, the hound dog from the farm spotted him.

"Simon, farmer Fred has been worried sick! Hurry, hurry, come home quick," said Davie.

"When we share our gifts with others,

God will make sure our needs are covered," said Davie.

So, Simon agreed to go back to the farm.

" I can be brave.

I can be strong.

God will take care of me, to
Him I belong."

Sheering day was here, and Simon was ready to be brave.

THE END

CPSIA information can be obtained
at www.ICGtesting.com
Printed in the USA
LVHW071058100821
695003LV00003B/73

9 781737 223214